New Jersey
History

Mark Stewart

Heinemann Library
Chicago, Illinois

© 2004 Heinemann Library
a division of Reed Elsevier Inc.
Chicago, Illinois

Customer Service 888-454-2279

Visit our website at www.heinemannlibrary.com

Designed by Heinemann Library
Page layout by Wilkinson Design
Printed and bound in the United States by
    Lake Book Manufacturing, Inc.

08 07 06 05 04
10 9 8 7 6 5 4 3 2 1

**Library of Congress
Cataloging-in-Publication Data**

Stewart, Mark, 1960-
  New Jersey history / Mark Stewart.
      v. cm.
  Includes bibliographical references and index.
  Contents: Early New Jersey (up to 1700) --
New Jersey and the new
nation (1700/1781) -- A nation divided
(1781/1900) -- A new century (1900/1950) --
Toward the new millennium (1950/present) --
Map of New Jersey -- Timeline.
    ISBN 1-4034-0673-1 (HC library binding) --
ISBN 1-4034-2683-X (PB)
  1. New Jersey--History--Juvenile literature.
[1. New Jersey--History.]
I. Title.
  F134.3.S75 2003
  974.9--dc21
                                        2003009429

Acknowledgments

The author and publishers are grateful to the
following for permission to reproduce copyright
material:

Cover photographs by (main) The Granger
Collection, New York (row, L-R) Baldwin H.
Ward & Kathryn C. Ward/Corbis, The Granger
Collection, New York, Corbis, Charles E.
Rotkin/Corbis

Title page (L-R) Kelly-Mooney Photography/Corbis,
The Granger Collection, New York, The Granger
Collection, New York; contents page, pp. 6, 10,
18, 22, 24 The Granger Collection, New York;
pp. 4, 27, 32, 34, 35, 39 Bettmann/Corbis; pp. 7,
9, 14, 29 North Wind Picture Archives; pp. 12, 16,
40 Lee Snider/Corbis; pp. 15, 30, 31, 33 Corbis;
pp. 20, 28 New Jersey Historical Society; p. 36
Roger Wood/Corbis; pp. 37, 38 Charles E. Rotkin/
Corbis; p. 41T Hector Emmanuel/Heinemann
Library; p. 41B Richard T. Nowitz/Corbis; p. 43
Kelly-Mooney Photography/Corbis

Photo research by John Klein

Special thanks to expert reader Chad Leinaweaver,
the Director for the Library at The New Jersey
Historical Society, for his help in the preparation
of this book.

Every effort has been made to contact copyright
holders of any material reproduced in this book.
Any omissions will be rectified in subsequent
printings if notice is given to the publisher.

Some words are shown in bold, **like this.**
You can find out what they mean by looking
in the glossary.

Contents

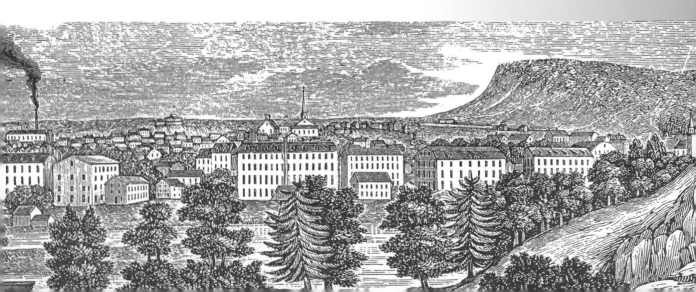

Early New Jersey: Prehistory to 1700

Each state in our nation has a story to tell about its land and people. New Jersey's story includes Native Americans, explorers, colonists, wars, progress, and even problems. These are all a part of New Jersey's history.

New Jersey's earliest history can be traced to the native people who lived there for thousands of years. The first humans to make what we now call New Jersey their home were the **Paleo-Indians.** These people arrived in New Jersey about 12,000 years ago. The Paleo-Indians lived near forests, next to rivers, and along the seashore.

This drawing of one of New Jersey's earliest inhabitants shows how they might have dressed.

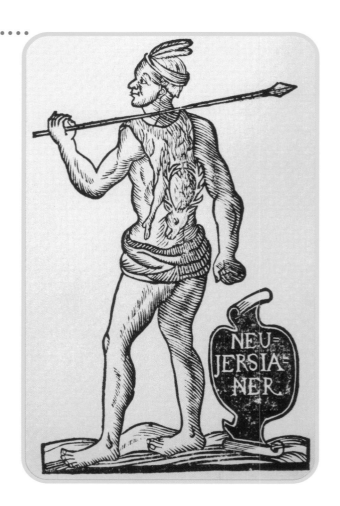

They hunted large animals, such as **mammoths.** They also fished and gathered mussels. About 1,000 years ago, they began to farm. Those farmers were the **ancestors** of the people who call themselves the Lenni Lenape.

THE LENNI LENAPE: C.E. 1000

The name *Lenape* has a number of different translations, including "genuine people," "original people," and "our men." The Lenape people are also known as the Delaware. *Delaware* is the English name given to the Lenape by European settlers. That name was taken from the Delaware River, which flowed through the Lenape's land. The Lenape were members of the Algonquin nation. The Algonquins lived in much of what is now New England and the Mid-Atlantic region.

To locate places in New Jersey, turn to the map on page 44.

The Lenape had long black hair and a tall, shapely appearance. On average, they were taller than the European settlers who first encountered them in the 1500s. They were a peaceful people who farmed, hunted, and fished for food, and who helped the early European explorers and settlers. They called the land where they lived *Scheyechbi*, which meant "land along water."

Three different Lenape groups lived in New Jersey—the Munsee, Unami, and Unalachtigo. The Munsee lived in the northern part of New Jersey, the Unami in the central areas, and the Unalachtigo in the south. The lakes and rivers of the north and the ocean **inlets** and **estuaries** of the south supplied plenty of food. The Lenni Lenape also used these bodies of water to travel and trade.

EARLY EUROPEAN EXPLORERS: 1498–1609

The first European explorers came to New Jersey by way of the Atlantic Ocean, which borders New Jersey to the east. The explorers were looking for a shorter route from Europe to Asia. At that time, European merchants could become very wealthy by bringing over spices and other goods from Asia and selling them in Europe. It was in their best interest to find the shortest route possible between the two continents.

English ships first spotted New Jersey's coast in 1497 or 1498, but the sailors did not land or make contact with the native people at that time. Captain John Cabot, an Italian explorer working for the English, claimed New Jersey's coastal lands for King Henry VII.

In 1524, Giovanni da Verrazzano, an Italian explorer who worked for the French, sailed along the New Jersey coast and saw people waving to him from shore. It was during this expedition that New Jersey was put on a map for the first time.

Henry Hudson, pictured below, also sailed up the Hudson River and along the coast of New York.

In 1609, Henry Hudson, exploring for the **Dutch East India Company,** anchored his ships in what are now Sandy Hook Bay and Newark Bay. This was the first time Europeans actually explored New Jersey's land. Hudson claimed the land for the Dutch. In 1620, another Dutch explorer, Cornelius Mey, explored the Delaware River. Cape May, which forms the southern tip of New Jersey, is named after him.

EUROPEAN SETTLEMENT: 1620–1700

The first European settlers in the region were Dutch. They came from the Netherlands in Europe. They claimed the land based on Henry

In the Netherlands, the Dutch often built windmills with six sides. When they came to New Jersey, they sometimes used this design for other buildings. This meeting house in Burlington also has six sides.

Hudson's discoveries. The colony was called New Netherland, and it included parts of what are now the states of New Jersey, Connecticut, Delaware, and New York.

In the 1620s, Dutch settlers started a trading post near present-day Albany on the Hudson River. A second post, called New Amsterdam, was started at the southern tip of Manhattan Island. The settlers had discovered that the local Native Americans were excellent hunters, and they began trading European-made alcohol, cloth, and guns for animal **pelts.** The pelts were then taken back to Europe and sold for a large **profit.**

Patroons

When New Netherland was founded, it was run by the Dutch East India Company. The company's sole purpose was to make money, and the laws the colonists had to follow were actually the company's laws.

In 1628, the company came up with a patroonship plan. Under this plan, the company would give an individual—the patroon—a large piece of land. The patroon would then spend his own money convincing settlers to come and farm on his land. He was permitted to govern the settlers as he saw fit.

An American Classic?

Finnish settlers came to New Netherland in the 1600s. They brought with them something that many people think of as purely American: the log cabin!

In 1630, the Dutch established their first settlements in New Jersey, across the harbor from Manhattan, in present-day Hoboken and Jersey City. The Dutch settlements in New Jersey had no name. For three decades, the Dutch thought of them as part of New Amsterdam. This changed in 1660, when a group of farming families decided to build a village protected by log walls. They named it *Bergen*, Dutch for "the hills," and built the state's first church and first schoolhouse. Today, Bergen is located within Jersey City.

Soon Dutch farmers began settling other parts of New Jersey. They pushed westward along the major inland rivers and established the villages of Hackensack, Passaic, and New Brunswick. The Dutch farmers favored the land in New Jersey to other places. It reminded them of their homeland in the Netherlands. The **climate** was similar, there were rivers and forests, and the soil was rich. That rich soil was very important to New Jersey's early farmers. They were able to grow and then sell boatloads of fruits and vegetables. This helped the New Netherland colony survive.

From early colonial times, people came to New Netherland from a variety of countries, including present-day Germany, Sweden, and Finland. At that time, none came for political or religious reasons. They all came to make money. About twenty different languages were spoken in the colony. In fact, historians estimate that as much as one half of the entire population of New Netherland was not Dutch.

Swedish settlers attempted to start a colony along the western edge of the Delaware River in 1641. Called New Sweden, it was the only Swedish colony started in

America. A man named Johan Printz governed New Sweden. Printz weighed 400 pounds and was nearly seven feet tall. No one dared defy him, and he ruled with a stern hand for a decade.

By 1655, the Dutch wanted to expand into western New Jersey. They sent ships carrying 300 soldiers to the colony of New Sweden, which surrendered as soon as the soldiers came ashore. Sweden gave up all its claims to the region, but the Dutch invited Finnish and Swedish farmers to stay in the area.

While governor of New Sweden, Printz established good relations with the Lenni Lenape and developed trade with the settlers of New Netherland.

The Netherlands continued to govern the region until 1664, when the English sent a military force to take it away. The English saw how **prosperous** New Netherland had become, and they decided they wanted it for themselves. England said that John Cabot's earlier claim to the region gave them control of the area. The Dutch were **shrewd** traders, but they could not match the power of England's navy. The Netherlands gave New Amsterdam and the Dutch settlements around it to England without a fight.

The English renamed New Netherland. They called it New York, in honor of the king's brother James, the Duke of York. In 1664, the Duke of York gave the land between the Delaware and Hudson Rivers to two of his friends, Lord John Berkeley and Sir George Carteret. The Duke then renamed this land New Jersey, after the Isle of Jersey. The Isle of Jersey is located off the

This engraving shows Philip Carteret arriving in New Jersey in 1665. His argument with the English colonial governor of New York, Edmund Andros, led to his brief imprisonment.

English coast and was governed by George Carteret at the time. Carteret and Berkeley agreed to send George's relative, Philip Carteret, to govern New Jersey.

Philip Carteret wanted to make sure the settlements established in New Jersey would grow. To attract people, he arranged for them to buy land at a very reasonable price. He promised they could follow any religion they chose. Carteret believed that the people of New Jersey should make their own laws. It was Carteret who created New Jersey's first **assembly** in 1668.

New Jersey's rich soil attracted thousands of people from other English colonies in Connecticut, Long Island, and Massachusetts. The **economy** of the colony

This farmhouse, built in 1676 at Lyons Farms, New Jersey, was typical of many built during that time.

depended almost entirely on farming. In 1666, a group from Connecticut founded the town of Newark. During the same period, the towns of Middletown and Shrewsbury were founded near the ocean to the south.

For the most part, the families moving to New Jersey came from the more established New England colonies. Many were **Puritans,** who had originally come to the colonies so they would be free to practice their religion. In the 1670s, members from another religious group called the **Quakers** began sailing to New Jersey directly from England. They settled near the Delaware River in southern and western New Jersey. They established the towns of Burlington and Salem.

In 1674, the Quakers—with the help of William Penn—bought John Berkeley's share of New Jersey. A few years later, the colony was divided into two parts—West Jersey and East Jersey. West Jersey was the first Quaker colony in America. George Carteret owned East Jersey until he died in 1680. After his death, a

A Royal Province

Following the death of George Carteret, East Jersey was sold at auction to twelve Quakers, one of whom was William Penn. Each of these 12 people sold half their share of the land to another, and so East Jersey came to have 24 owners. They chose Robert Barclay, a Scotch Quaker, to be governor for life. Later, people challenged their claim to the land. In 1702, the whole colony was surrendered to England. New Jersey became a royal province.

This Episcopal church in Burlington, New Jersey, is the oldest Episcopal church in the state. It was built in 1703 and still stands today.

different group of Quakers, called the Twenty-Four **Proprietors,** bought East Jersey. They were led by William Penn.

East Jersey's **capital** was Perth Amboy, at the mouth of the Raritan River. West Jersey's capital was the town of Burlington, a village on the Delaware River. Life in East Jersey focused on community, with people living near one another and working together. In West Jersey, where the farms were larger and the population smaller, people might go a week without talking to or seeing a neighbor. New Jersey remained divided until 1702.

In 1682, the Lenape Indians had signed a **treaty** of friendship with William Penn. Despite the treaty, however, colonists began to push inland into Lenape territory. The Lenape were driven from their lands. Many died from European diseases, to which they had been exposed for the first time. In 1758, the British government created an area that would belong only to the Lenape. Those who had not been killed by warfare or disease were forced to live at the Brotherton **Reservation** near the present-day town of Indian Mills. This reservation was the first of its kind anywhere in the world.

A History of Road Building

New Jersey is famous for its seemingly countless number of roads and highways. The state's residents even make jokes about it. Few realize, however, that this reputation dates back to the 1600s.

In the years after British rule was established, New Jerseyans made road-building one of their most important projects. New Jersey lay between the important cities of New York and Philadelphia, so good land transportation was needed between the Hudson and Delaware Rivers. Laws were passed in the 1670s to ensure that New Jersey's towns were connected to one another. Many roads followed winding paths first created by the Lenni Lenape.

It took several decades to build New Jersey's first road system. Part of the problem was that people were often forced by the government to build or repair roads near their homes. But they were not paid to make repairs, so they did not work very hard. As a result, most of New Jersey's original roads were bumpy. It was easier to travel in the dead of winter, when snow covered the ground and a horse-drawn sleigh could be used.

By this time, life for New Jersey's European settlers was fairly pleasant. The same could not be said for the slaves of New Jersey. African slaves had been among the very first settlers of the region. After the British took over the land in 1664, they awarded settlers 75 acres of land for each slave the settler had. The African slaves worked hard without pay and with little hope of gaining their freedom. They were bought and sold in Perth Amboy, which was the colony's main port. By 1740, when New Jersey had a total population of almost 50,000, more than 3,000 of those people were African slaves.

Colonial New Jersey and the Road to Independence: 1700–1783

During the first 100 years of British rule, New Jersey's population grew to almost 200,000 people. From Newark, settlers pushed westward to start the towns of Orange and Morristown. From Salem and Burlington, people ventured north to establish Trenton and Camden. The discovery of **iron ore** led to the state's first **industrial** towns, such as Dover and Ringwood.

BUSINESS IN COLONIAL NEW JERSEY

During the **Industrial Revolution**, there was a great need for iron. **Industries** in Great Britain often used iron brought from the colonies. To meet British demand for iron, **foundries** in New Jersey worked night and day. The foundries needed hundreds of acres of wood each year to make fires hot enough to melt metal.

This foundry in Morristown, New Jersey, employed many workers and provided iron for Great Britain.

Forests were cleared of their trees, and much of New Jersey was turned into farmland. Cities such as Philadelphia to the west and New York to the east became the customers of colonial farmers in New Jersey. Other industries also developed in colonial New Jersey during the 1700s, especially grain **mills**, sawmills, and knitting mills.

THE FRENCH AND INDIAN WAR: 1754–1763

The colony of New Jersey experienced rapid growth and **economic** success. Great Britain wanted this success to spread beyond New Jersey. It wanted to expand westward, toward the Mississippi River. But France had already claimed that land. In 1753, war broke out between the two world powers. That war eventually spilled over into Europe.

Several major battles were waged in North America during the French and Indian War. Fighting took place along the frontier, where many settlers were killed. Although most of the battles took place outside of New Jersey's borders, there were raids along the Delaware River and some fighting in Sussex County. The war also created hardships of a different kind for many New Jerseyans. For the first time they were asked to directly support the British Crown. Some were asked for money. Others were asked to provide food and materials. A few were even asked to open their homes to provide shelter for British troops.

Good Thinking

Two of the nation's oldest colleges were founded in colonial New Jersey. In 1746, the College of New Jersey (now Princeton University) was established. Twenty years later, Queen's College (now Rutgers University) opened its doors.

The Old Barracks built in Trenton, New Jersey, in 1758, still stands today.

Many New Jersey colonists thought this was unfair. They felt that the war was between Great Britain and France, and had nothing to do with them. New Jerseyans did not want to pay for the war with their own hard-earned money. Their anger grew when, a few years later, the British tried to take over private homes in Newark, Perth Amboy, and Elizabethtown. The British wanted to use the homes to house hundreds of their soldiers. But New Jerseyans did not like this idea. Instead, they built five barracks, or buildings, to house the soldiers in Perth Amboy, Elizabethtown, New Brunswick, Burlington, and Trenton. The Old Barracks in Trenton is still standing.

REVOLUTIONARY WAR ERA: 1764–1783

After the French and Indian War ended in 1763, the British began taxing colonists. The tax was partly used to pay off Great Britain's **debts** from the long conflict. This seemed unfair to many colonists. But the colonists were mostly upset because they had no say in Great Britain's government. They did not have representatives in the government they were paying to support.

In New Jersey, as in other colonies, there was a growing movement to break free of Great Britain and declare

New Jersey's Signers

Five men from New Jersey signed the Declaration of Independence in 1776:

Abraham Clark

John Hart

Frances Hopkinson

Richard Stockton

John Witherspoon

independence. Several New Jerseyans worked hard to find a peaceful solution. They did not want a war with Great Britain. They knew that New Jersey's location would make it a dangerous place to live during a war. New Jersey was between the northern colonies and the southern colonies. Also, it was located between Philadelphia, the headquarters of the **Continental Congress,** and New York City, the center of British command during the war. There was almost no way to get from one region to the other without fighting right through the state.

Victories in New Jersey

Several key victories for the Continental Army took place in New Jersey:

Trenton	December 1776
Princeton	January 1777
Monmouth	June 1778
Springfield	June 1780

When war did come, New Jerseyans fought on both sides. Some, called Patriots, joined the Continental Army and fought for American independence. Others, called Loyalists, remained loyal to the British king. Still others did not support either side. Slaves and free African Americans also fought on both sides of the conflict, but more fought for the British. This was because the British promised freedom to any slaves who left their Patriot owners and fought for the British.

In the fall of 1776, the Continental Army, under the command of George Washington, arrived in New Jersey. After capturing a huge supply of American ammunition at Fort Lee, the British pushed the Continental Army across New Jersey to the Delaware River. The Continental Army used every boat it could find in western New Jersey and fled into Pennsylvania. The British, with no boats of their own, had to stop their pursuit and wait for the river to freeze so they could cross on foot. At this point, the British thought that they were going to win the war easily.

A ferry crossing was established at this point on the Delaware River around 1700. But the crossing was not known to many, and so was a perfect spot for Washington to cross with his troops.

They were sure that the long and cold winter would cripple the Continental forces.

On Christmas Eve, Washington assembled the Continental Army and they secretly crossed the Delaware River back into New Jersey. They marched through the pre-dawn hours toward Trenton, where there was a large force of **Hessian** soldiers who were being paid to fight for the

Three Constitutions

New Jersey's first state **constitution** was written during the Revolutionary War in 1776. It created the state's government. It was the only state constitution written during the Revolutionary War era that gave women the right to vote. Free African Americans and Native Americans were also given the right to vote. However, this right was taken away in 1807.

New Jersey's constitution has been rewritten twice since 1776. Leaders made changes because life in New Jersey had changed. In 1844, a **bill of rights** was added to the constitution. Also, the three branches of government were separated. The third constitution was written in 1947. Based on that constitution, the governor is now allowed to be in office for four years, not three. That version also reorganized the state's court system.

New Jersey Women of the Revolution

New Jersey women had different opinions about the Revolution. Some were Patriots. Others were Loyalists. Still others did not take sides. But no matter which side they supported, women faced special problems during that time.

When husbands, fathers, or adult sons left home to fight, women had two choices. They could stay and run the family farm or business. Or, they could follow the armies into battle. Women who stayed home not only had to continue running the household, making clothing, and preparing food for the family, they also had to work in the fields or run a business. These women, Patriot or Loyalist, also faced the possibility that soldiers might pass through town and demand their hard-earned food or supplies.

Women who followed the armies also faced difficulties. They had to march mile after mile on foot, make do with limited food, and often care for young children at the same time. They also did not know if they would have a home to return to. Life was difficult for New Jersey's women during the Revolution, but their spirit and determination carried them through the tough times.

British. The Continental Army took the Hessians by surprise. Nine hundred Hessians were captured, and over one hundred were killed or wounded. Only four men in the Continental Army were killed.

After another small battle at Trenton, the Continental Army marched north and east to Princeton. There, General Washington and the Continental Army faced British soldiers under the command of General Cornwallis at the Battle of Princeton. Washington then took his exhausted army to Morristown, where they camped for the winter. News of these victories spread and lifted the spirits of the colonists. Thousands of people volunteered for the Continental Army in 1777, and thousands more joined local **militias** to defend their land against the British.

In the spring of 1777, the British tried to force Washington's army out of the hilly region around Morristown.

This image shows the Battle of Springfield, which took place on June 23, 1780. The battle marked the last time that the British invaded New Jersey.

The British were used to fighting while standing in straight lines, exposed to whatever was facing them. They expected the Patriots to do the same. But local farmers surprised British troops by joining together in small bands, making quick attacks, and then retreating to the cover of the hills. The confused British withdrew to the Hudson River and boarded ships to Philadelphia. They felt the colonists had fought unfairly by not showing themselves. They also did not want to march across New Jersey anymore.

The New Jersey Militia and the Continental Army continued to make life miserable for the British. Men in small forts along the Delaware River fired upon any boats attempting to supply British troops in Philadelphia. The British fought to stop them for almost a year, and these efforts cost them valuable supplies and soldiers.

After a miserable winter at Valley Forge, Pennsylvania, General Washington returned to New Jersey with the Continental Army in 1778. They were chasing the British, who were marching to New York. Washington and his army caught them near Freehold. They fought the Battle

Colonel Tye

Titus was born a slave in Monmouth County, New Jersey. Although most slaves in that area had been freed by their **Quaker** owners, Titus remained in slavery. In November 1775, Titus escaped and went to live under the protection of the British.

Titus changed his name, and, as Colonel Tye, began leading raids against Patriot forces. During the Battle of Monmouth, he captured a captain of the Monmouth Militia. At one point, while leading the Black Brigade, he was in charge of close to one hundred men.

Colonel Tye was hit in the wrist by a musket ball during a raid in 1780. The wound became infected, and Tye died in September of that year.

of Monmouth on June 28, 1778. Neither side officially won. However, the Patriots learned that the British weren't unbeatable. After the battle, the British retreated. Local people chased the British and fired at them all the way to Sandy Hook, where they boarded ships to New York.

The Continental Army won the next major battle on New Jersey soil. In the spring of 1780, the British once again tried to remove the Continental Army from Morristown. The British outnumbered Washington's troops 5,000 to 2,500. But New Jersey's **minutemen** were prepared to take up arms beside the Continental Army. As the British advanced toward Morristown, a cannon fired a signal shot. Thousands of local minutemen grabbed their guns and streamed toward Springfield, where the two armies fought. Suddenly, it was the British who were outnumbered. After a day of fighting they were forced to retreat.

America won its independence in 1781. The people of New Jersey played a great role in that victory. The colony witnessed about 100 battles, both large and small. More than 15,000 New Jerseyans fought the British between 1775 and 1781. They were rewarded for their bravery with an independent country.

A Nation Divided: 1783–1900

In the years following the Revolutionary War, New Jerseyans struggled to return their lives to normal. For a brief time, the towns of Princeton and Trenton each served as the new nation's **capital.** Some people thought Trenton should be the permanent capital of the United States. It was easy to get to from both north and south, and it was almost exactly in the middle of the thirteen colonies. In the end, it was decided that the nation's seat of government should be in Washington, D.C. Trenton then became New Jersey's capital.

INDUSTRY

Industry changed much for the colonists after the war. Before the war, colonists bought products made in England, often from materials originally produced in the colonies. But after the war, Americans had to manufacture their own products. New Jersey's geographical location

The Passaic River and Falls, seen here in the foreground, provided energy that ran the mills of Paterson, New Jersey.

made it an ideal place to build factories. Its many rivers provided energy for various types of **mills.**

In 1791, a group called the Society for Establishing Useful Manufacturers selected a spot on the Passaic River, just below picturesque Great Falls, to build a town of factories. The fast-running water was channeled into large mills, where it provided power by turning enormous wheels. Workers lived in homes built nearby. The city was named Paterson in honor of New Jersey's governor, William Paterson. The Paterson experiment was a huge success. Within a few years, similar factory towns sprang up all over the state, producing everything from textiles to flour to leather to lumber.

The new factories and mills created jobs for many New Jerseyans, including women and children. Children as young as ten worked long hours every day. The workers were often hurt on the job. Many factory owners were concerned only with the amount of money they could make. They did not care about the safety of the workplaces or the health of their workers.

In 1828, workers at a silk mill in Paterson, New Jersey, went on **strike.** Among the strikers were many children. The strikers told the mill owner that they would not work until the number of hours they worked each day were reduced. In 1835, 1,500 children who worked in a cotton mill went on strike. The children were working as many as 60 hours a week. This did not leave them time to attend school or be with their families. Employers often called in the police to quiet the strikers. Men, women, and children continued to strike throughout the next 100 years. Workers and employers struggled to find a balance that allowed workers to be treated fairly, yet allowed the employers to make a **profit.**

The Delaware and Raritan Canal was completed in 1834. This engraving shows a length of the canal at Bound Brook, New Jersey, in 1844.

TRANSPORTATION

Goods created in New Jersey's factory towns followed the same path as the fruits and vegetables grown in the state. They would travel over land to the big markets in New York City and Philadelphia. In the early 1800s, new methods of moving goods—including the fast-moving steamboat—came to New Jersey. The nation's first oceangoing steamboat made regular trips from the city of Hoboken around the southern tip of New Jersey to Philadelphia.

Another way goods were moved was by large, flat boats called barges. These moved through a system of **canals.** There were two canal systems in New Jersey. The first was the Morris Canal, which connected the Hudson River at Jersey City to the Delaware River 100 miles away in Phillipsburg. Because the Delaware River was much higher than the Hudson, a series of 23 ramps were built and ropes were used to pull barges higher every few miles.

The Delaware and Raritan Canal connected the Raritan River at New Brunswick to the Delaware River at Bordentown. This canal used a series of locks to deal with the difference in altitude between the two main bodies of water. This cut the time it took to take a trip from New York to Philadelphia by three or four days.

As New Jersey's **economy** grew, demand increased for the goods it produced. The idea of moving people and products by rail was just coming into fashion during this time, but New Jerseyans were divided on whether or not to build a railroad. In the 1820s, the first locomotives were slow and inefficient. John Stevens, a Hoboken inventor, had a powerful 10-ton locomotive made in England and shipped back across the Atlantic. It was too heavy to run on wooden tracks, so his son, John, invented an iron rail that could be laid across wooden ties and secured with heavy iron spikes. This system is still in use today.

In 1833, New Jersey christened its first railroad line, the Camden & Amboy. It reduced the time it took to travel between Philadelphia and New York to a mere seven

The Steamboat Monopoly

In 1808, Robert Fulton and Robert Livingston were granted a **monopoly** from the state of New York state to operate steamboats on the state's waterways. This allowed them to run steamboats on the waterways of New York, especially the Hudson River, but also on bodies of water that stretched between states. This monopoly was very important because steamboats, which carried both people and goods, made money for the people who ran the boats.

Problems arose when the right to use a waterway was given by different authorities. For example, a steamboat operator named Aaron Ogden operated steamboats between New Jersey and New York. However, another man named Thomas Gibbons also used this same route. The United States Supreme Court had to decide which operator had the right to run his steamboats. It decided that the waterways should be open to all steamboats.

New Jersey Transportation, mid-1800s

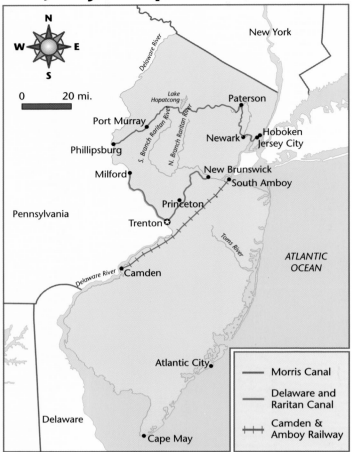

New Jersey's canals and railways were connected to natural rivers and lakes, creating a far-reaching transportation system.

hours. Railroad travel became so popular that by the mid-1800s, there were over a dozen different companies operating lines in the state.

IMMIGRATION

By the mid-1800s, New Jersey's population was changing greatly. With the sudden rise of factories, canal-building, and railroads, there was a desperate need for all kinds of workers, from engineers and scientists to miners and canal-diggers. European **immigrants** from countries such as Germany, Wales, and Ireland came to New Jersey. Many women—mostly young and unmarried—also joined the growing workforce in large numbers.

CIVIL WAR, 1861–1865

New Jersey and other northern states had grown **economically** strong during the early years of America's **Industrial Revolution.** But southern states continued to make most of their money through agriculture. They came to rely more and more on slave labor to meet the North's increasing demand for **raw materials** and agricultural goods. But there was a strong movement in the North to abolish slavery. Among its most vocal opponents were New Jersey's **Quakers,** who opposed slavery for religious reasons. Despite these strong antislavery voices, however, New Jersey was the last Northern state to abolish slavery, in 1846. And, it was the

only Northern state to vote against Abraham Lincoln, who was opposed to slavery, in the 1860 and 1864 presidential elections.

During the Industrial Revolution, factories in the cities of Trenton, Newark, Paterson, and Camden swelled with immigrant workers from Ireland, Germany, and Italy.

Tensions increased between the North and South during the 1850s. By 1861, eleven southern states had broken away from the United States and formed the Confederate States of America. The Civil War had begun. On May 6, 1861, New Jersey became the first Northern state to send troops and supplies to Washington, D.C.

With hundreds of thousands of soldiers fighting, the need for everything from boots to bullets to boats kept New Jersey's factories humming. Cities like Paterson and

From Station to Station

During the 1850s, some newcomers to New Jersey did not stay long at all. They were slaves escaping from the South. Many fugitive slaves did not wish to stay in New Jersey, because the state cooperated with the South by returning runaway slaves. But despite this, New Jersey had several so-called stations on the **Underground Railroad** that helped slaves gain their freedom. Among the cities where the escaped slaves could find food, shelter, and a conductor, or guide, to their next stop were Camden, New Brunswick, and Paterson. From 1849 to 1852, the legendary Underground Railroad leader Harriet Tubman spent much of her time in southern New Jersey. When she was not helping with escapes, she often worked in hotels in Cape May to earn money for the Underground Railroad.

Nurse Cornelia Hancock

Cornelia Hancock, from Salem, New Jersey, was able to follow a New Jersey regiment into battle during the Civil War. She acted as a nurse. This is part of a letter she wrote home on July 7, 1863, after the Battle of Gettysburg.

I am very tired tonight: having been in the field all day.... There are no words in the English language to express the suffering I witnessed today.... The men lie on the ground; their clothes have been cut off them to dress their wounds.... I would get on first rate if they would not ask me to write to their wives; that I cannot do without crying.... I do not mind the sight of blood, having seen limbs taken off and was not sick at all. Women [nurses] are needed here badly ... but nothing short of an [official] order ... will let you through the battle lines.

Camden grew strong during the Civil War, and business owners there became extremely wealthy. In the end, the North's ability to manufacture more supplies than the South played an important role in the North's victory. New Jersey was a big part of that. Almost every New Jerseyan was involved in the war in some way, whether he or she worked in a factory, grew food, or actually fought. Of the million-plus men who joined the Union Army between 1861 and 1865, 88,000 were from New Jersey. More than 6,000 New Jerseyans lost their lives in battle.

The 2nd New Jersey Cavalry was organized on August 15, 1863. They fought in Mississippi, Alabama, Georgia, and Tennessee.

THE POSTWAR PERIOD

In the years following the Civil War, New Jersey continued to expand its economic influence and might. Much of the state's success was tied to the booming population centers of New York and Philadelphia. As **immigrants** poured into those cities in increasing numbers, they looked to New Jersey for food, clothing, and other goods.

Life in New Jersey's Pine Barrens was tough. The people who settled there developed a reputation for being hard workers.

Many of these new Americans crossed the Delaware and Hudson Rivers and put down roots in New Jersey. Most were from eastern and southern Europe. They first settled in the state during the 1860s, when land speculators hoped to turn the Pine Barrens into productive farmland. Italian farmers knew how to work with poor soil, and many came to the United States just for this purpose. Twenty years later, thousands of Italians were coming to work New Jersey farms each year.

Most immigrants to the United States came through Ellis Island, in New York Harbor. Many then went to New Jersey. As a result, cities such as Newark, Elizabeth, Jersey City, Paterson, Passaic, and Hoboken were a **melting pot** of people from different countries.

Constitutional Amendments

After the Civil War, New Jersey at first refused to ratify the Thirteenth, Fourteenth, and Fifteenth Amendments to the U.S. **Constitution.** These are the amendments that ban slavery and give men of different races equal rights in the United States. Many New Jerseyans sympathized with the South and its problems.

Amendment:	Date Ratified by the U.S.:
Thirteenth	1865
Fourteenth	1868
Fifteenth	1870

A Century of Change: 1900–1970

As the 1900s began, New Jersey's **industrial** might was greater than ever. World War I (1914–1918) broke out in Europe in 1914, and the United States entered the war in 1917. New Jersey's factories found ways to further increase their production. One of the busiest places in the world during this time was Hoboken. The city's docks were full of activity as soldiers and supplies were loaded on ships bound for Europe. Nearly half the Americans who fought in Europe left from Hoboken.

The war boosted the fortunes of many New Jersey businesses. A number of companies retooled their machines to create military items. For example, the Singer Company—located in Elizabeth—stopped

Hoboken greeted American soldiers returning from World War I. These soldiers cheer on the deck of the Agamemnon *upon their return from war in 1919.*

making sewing machines and began making parts for weapons. One business that benefited greatly was the chemical industry. With Germany as an enemy in World War I, America found itself suddenly cut off from many of the important chemicals that country produced. Several chemical companies in New Jersey discovered the Germans' secrets, and this made the state one of the biggest chemical-producers in the world.

The Great Migration

Between 1915 and 1920, about 500,000 African Americans left their jobs on farms in the south and moved to the industrial north. Thousands came to work in the factories of New Jersey. They took jobs that had been left open by men who had been called to fight in World War I. They were paid more for these manufacturing jobs than they had received while working in the south.

Throughout the 1920s, jobs in New Jersey were plentiful and people there lived well. Automobiles became affordable for almost anyone to buy. Tens of thousands of New Jerseyans who had never ventured more than a few miles from home began driving all over the state. The Jersey shore, with its 100-plus miles of magnificent beaches between Cape May and Sandy Hook, became immensely popular during this time.

With more cars came the need for more and better roads. By the 1920s, dozens of road improvement

During the 1920s, many New Jerseyans attended health classes along the state's wide beaches.

The 19th Amendment

Women in New Jersey had enjoyed the right to vote from 1776 through 1807, when a new state **constitution** took that right away. For 113 years, New Jersey women gave speeches, sent letters, and signed petitions while trying to regain their lost voting rights. Their efforts were finally rewarded in 1920, when the passage of the 19th Amendment gave women across the United States the right to vote.

programs were under way. Indeed, in the early days of automobile travel, no state spent more time and money improving its roads than New Jersey. Over the next two decades, several road features familiar to every American first appeared in the state, including clover leaf highway exits and jug handle turns.

Building Bridges

The state's first major bridge project, the Benjamin Franklin Bridge, was completed in 1926. It spanned the Delaware River, linking the cities of Camden and Philadelphia. A year later, the Holland Tunnel was completed, followed by the George Washington Bridge in 1931 and the Lincoln Tunnel in 1937. Before these projects, the only way to get  across the water to Manhattan was by ferry boat or through railroad tunnels built before World War I (1914–1918). The Hudson River bridges and tunnels strengthened the link between New Jersey and New York City and tempted many city dwellers to leave the crowds of Manhattan behind for the rolling hills in the northern and central parts of New Jersey.

THE GREAT DEPRESSION

The Great Depression of the 1930s hit New Jersey very hard. The images of this period often show poor people begging in cities, but farmers had it just as bad. During the boom years of the 1920s, New Jersey's farmers expanded their operations, even if they had to borrow the money to do it. When the **economy** slowed and demand for their produce dropped, they could not sell their fruits, vegetables, and dairy products for enough money to repay their loans. Hundreds of big farms went out of business, and this dragged down New Jersey's whole economy.

Soon the state's **mills** and factories began closing. With more people out of work, many stores could not afford to stay open. What had once been busy, vibrant villages and cities suddenly looked like ghost towns. The government started a number of programs aimed at keeping people working and giving relief to the poor. The programs were part of a plan called the New

Farmers suffered along with everyone else during the Great Depression. This migrant girl has managed to find work picking at a cranberry bog.

Deal, started by President Franklin D. Roosevelt. New Jersey benefited from government programs such as the Works Progress Administration and Civilian Conservation Corps. These programs recruited unemployed workers to build highways, bridges, buildings and do other public works. Many of these public works structures are still standing today.

WORLD WAR II: 1939–1945

World War II began in Europe 1939, but the United States did not enter the war until 1941. On December 7, 1941, Japan had attacked Pearl Harbor, in Hawaii. The United States was soon fighting Germany and Japan, and demand grew for all types of military items. This put New Jersey's factories, farms, and shipyards back in action, and its people back to work. The laborers this time around were a little different from those who answered the call during World War I (1914–1918). With half a million New Jersey men called into military service, women

At Fort Dix, future soldiers learned to use military equipment. These recruits are practicing a drill in their gas masks in 1941.

Many women worked in factories during World War II. This woman is assembling airplane parts at the Brewster Aeronautical Corporation in Newark.

entered the workforce in huge numbers. More African Americans also moved to New Jersey at this time. Between 1940 and 1950, New Jersey's African-American population grew by 40 percent.

New Jersey contributed to the war effort in other important ways. Once again, it served as a port for soldiers heading to Europe. It also was a training ground for new enlistees. At bases such as Fort Dix and Camp Kilmer, thousands of soldiers learned how to fight for their country. At Fort Hancock on Sandy Hook, gunners kept a wary eye on the Atlantic Ocean. It was their job to prevent German submarines from entering New York Harbor.

World War II ended in 1945 and the soldiers returned.

Seabrook Farms

During World War II, the New Jersey farms of the C. F. Seabrook family supplied U.S. troops with fresh and frozen food. But with so many troops fighting overseas, the family needed to find other workers. C. F.'s son, Jack, solved the problem by employing Japanese Americans who had been put in **internment camps** by the federal government.

Millions of cars have used the New Jersey Turnpike since it opened in 1952. Here, cars line up at a tollbooth in 1961.

New Jersey began a change that, in many ways, is still continuing today. During the 1950s, manufacturing in New Jersey grew even more. Factories made products ranging from cars to cookies to chemicals. People wanted to buy goods, and the state was more than happy to provide them. To keep pace with the competition, New Jersey companies recruited some of the country's top business minds and best technical people. The state government supported **industry** by passing laws that gave advantages to the big companies.

As manufacturing grew, the state's small towns began growing into major suburban centers. In areas that had been farmed for 200 years, residential areas began to rise. To get people from their homes to their jobs and to move goods into, out of, and through the state, New Jersey spent billions of dollars on new roads and highways. The New Jersey Turnpike, a major highway through the Northeast, opened in 1952. The Garden State Parkway, a 180-mile highway for passenger cars, opened in 1953. To get people into and out of the state, Newark's airport—which opened in 1929—underwent a series of expansions. Today, Newark Liberty is one of the busiest airports in the world.

In many states where the population grows rapidly, the farming business suffers. This was not the case in New Jersey. Throughout the 1900s, agriculture grew alongside other industries. Developments in the way food was grown, harvested, packed, preserved, and shipped helped New Jersey's farmers.

New Jersey continued to grow strong in the postwar decades. But during the 1960s and 1970s, it became clear that the state was not always growing with long-term concerns in mind. Pollution became a big problem. New Jerseyans were producing far more garbage than the state could handle, and many businesses were fouling the water and air. By the late 1960s, the Garden State could not boast of a very garden-like atmosphere.

New Jersey's problems were not limited to pollution. The move to the suburbs after World War II (1939–1945) had emptied cities such as Newark, Paterson, Camden, and Jersey City of strong

Smoke spews into the air from an industrial site in Newark, New Jersey, in 1965.

The formerly grand resort hotels of Atlantic City became run-down during the 1960s and 1970s. Later, they would be renovated and tourists would again come in droves.

businesses. In many neighborhoods, the elderly and poor now made up most of the population. They could not support local stores, which shut down or moved away. City factories too old to modernize could no longer compete and were also forced to close their doors.

Faced with mounting unemployment and crime, New Jersey's cities tumbled into near-ruin during the 1970s. Even the once-popular shore cities of Long Branch, Asbury Park, and Atlantic City fell into decay. Although life in the suburbs was as sweet as ever, state residents faced grave challenges in the final years of the 1900s.

CIVIL RIGHTS

During the 1960s, the **Civil Rights** movement gained attention through nonviolent acts such as marches and protests. But some clashes in New Jersey became violent. In July of 1967, a week-long riot broke out in Newark after white police officers mistreated a black cab driver. During the riot, 24 African-American citizens were killed, along with one white police officer and one white firefighter. The city was placed under the control of the state police and the national guard. It took a long time for things to return to normal. Some people say Newark was never the same again.

Three years after the riot, Kenneth Gibson became Newark's first African-American mayor. Although the city continued to suffer through difficult **economic** times, Gibson and the city leaders who followed him slowly restored Newark. By the end of the century, the city's future was looking bright for the first time in a long time.

Civil Rights activists demonstrate at the Democratic National Convention in Atlantic City in 1964.

Toward a New Millennium: 1970 to Present

The dramatic decline of New Jersey's **urban** areas in the 1970s served as a warning to other places that wanted rapid growth. But in the 1980s, New Jersey began to **thrive** again. New Jersey considered a number of ways it could recover. The state decided that the smartest way was to rely on the strength of its people.

TIME FOR RENEWAL

The state was able to recover because it reshaped itself to suit the demands of the times and the needs of all New Jerseyans. Businesses took on new technologies that created high-paying jobs. **Industries** such as telecommunications, insurance, and healthcare gained new momentum. They did well in New Jersey because of its people and business rules, and also because of its location between New York City and Philadelphia. New industrial centers replaced old ones. The state's **suburbs** once again grew.

*During the 1980s, cities such as Newark began a period of regrowth. Sparkling office towers were built and the **economy** thrived.*

As property prices rose, people looking for inexpensive homes turned to the state's crumbling cities. Long-forgotten towns such as Hoboken and Jersey City sprang back to life. Cities such as Newark and Camden started to rebound, and they drew new residents. In other parts of the state, towns were able to build new schools and upgrade public facilities.

Towns such as Hoboken thrived during the 1980s and 1990s. Here, people enjoy the weather at an outdoor restaurant.

New Jersey's problems did not magically go away, but the improvements that were made were far-reaching. The pollution problem was tackled first. Strict laws were passed to prevent further pollution of the ground, water, and air. The rules were tightly enforced. New Jersey's beaches—for years strewn with washed-up garbage—and beach towns returned to their former glory.

Today, New Jersey's beaches are clean again. They are enjoyed by thousands of people each summer.

The Newest New Jerseyans

Credit for New Jersey's recent successes belongs to every resident—including the 250,000 new **immigrants** that have streamed into the state since

the mid-1990s. They hail from South and Central America, Asia, India, Eastern Europe, and the Caribbean.

They follow a path similar to that of new arrivals 100 years ago—with some important differences. Banking and labor laws that were not in place back then mean these newcomers can buy a piece of the American dream as soon as they are ready. Many purchase homes or start businesses after just a few years in the state.

BOOM TIME

When America's **economy** started to boom in the 1990s, New Jersey was in the right place at the right time. The state's status as a modern and convenient air, sea, and ground transportation hub made it a crossroads of goods coming into the country, going out of the country, or just passing through.

The state also became home to hundreds of thousands of new residents. Wealthy people from New York City and Philadelphia came to New Jersey. Immigrants from all over the world arrived in New Jersey. In fact,

Today's New Jerseyans are taking advantage of their revitalized cities. They are busy creating their own histories.

from 1990 to 2000, over 500,000 immigrants made New Jersey their home. They brought further **diversity** to a state that has always opened its arms to new people.

It took nearly 400 years for New Jersey to become the state it is today. No one knows for sure how New Jersey will change in this century. But by applying the lessons learned during good times and bad, New Jerseyans can look forward to things to come.

Sporting Firsts

The study of sports in America brings historians back to New Jersey again and again. In 1846, the first official game of baseball was played in the town of Hoboken. In 1864, the first race, or derby, for three-year-old horses was held in Paterson. In 1869, the first college football game was played in New Brunswick, between Rutgers and Princeton. In 1899, the Trenton Nationals won the first professional basketball title. The first golf tee was invented by a South Orange dentist in 1921. And the first perfect game in the history of the Little League World Series was hurled by Freddy Shapiro of Delaware Township in 1956.

Map of New Jersey

N
W   E
S

0   20 mi.

Delaware River

Lake Hopatcong

S. Branch Raritan River

N. Branch Raritan River

Mahwah
Passaic
Hackensack
Wayne
Paterson
Paramus
Teaneck
West Orange
Fort Lee
Livingston
North Bergen
Morristown
Hoboken
Newark
Jersey City
Elizabeth
Bayonne
Piscataway
Plainfield
Edison
Perth Amboy
New Brunswick
Sandy Hook
Matawan
Princeton
Red Bank
Holmdel
Ewing
Long Branch
Trenton
Asbury Park

Willingboro
Toms River
Lakehurst
Camden
Browns Mills
Point Pleasant
Cherry Hill
Haddonfield
Marlton
Barnegat

Delaware River

Long Beach Island

Vineland

Millville
ATLANTIC OCEAN

Atlantic City
Ocean City
Avalon

Villas

Cape May

New York

Pennsylvania

New Jersey

Atlantic Ocean

Delaware

Timeline

C.E. **1000**	The Lenni Lenape Indians are living in New Jersey.
1497	Explorer John Cabot sees the coast of New Jersey from his ship and claims the land for England.
1524	Giovanni da Verrazzano sails along the New Jersey coast; for the first time, New Jersey is placed on a map.
1609	Henry Hudson claims New Jersey for the Dutch.
1630	Dutch colonists begin to settle New Jersey; their colony is called New Netherland.
1641	The Swedish colony of New Sweden is started on the Delaware River.
1664	England takes control of New Netherland and changes its name.
1670s	Many **Quakers** arrive in New Jersey. The colony continues to prosper.
1754–1763	The French and Indian War is fought. There are raids along the Delaware.
1758	All remaining Lenni Lenape are forced to move to a **reservation.**
1775–1783	The Revolutionary War is fought. Many key battles take place in New Jersey.
1776	New Jersey's first state **constitution** is written. Women, as well as free African Americans and Native Americans, have the right to vote. That right is taken away in 1807.
1790s	Factory towns spring up along New Jersey's rivers and falls.
1833	New Jersey's first railroad, the Camden & Amboy, is built.
1834	The Delaware and Raritan Canal is completed. Steamboats carry people and goods quickly to their destinations.
1861–1865	The Civil War is fought. New Jersey sides with the North.
1870	African-American men receive the right to vote.
1870s	Thousands of immigrants arrive in New Jersey.
1917	The United States enters World War I. Many soldiers pass through New Jersey.
1920	Women receive the right to vote.
1929	The Great Depression starts; New Jersey's **economy** struggles.
1941	The United States enters World War II. New Jersey men fight overseas while women move into their jobs in factories.
1950s	Manufacturing grows, highways are built, and suburbs are developed.
1960s	The Civil Rights movement takes place.
1970s	New Jersey's cities decline.
1980s	New **industries** are developed. Cities are rebuilt and experience growth.
2000	The economy is strong, and immigrants bring new **diversity** to New Jersey.

Glossary

ancestor relative who lived years before, such as a great-great grandmother

assembly group of people who make laws

bill of rights summary of fundamental rights, such as freedom of speech, guaranteed to people against violation of a government

canal human-made body of water joining two larger bodies of water

capital location of a government

civil rights basic rights of a citizen of a country, especially the right to be free from unfair control by the government or by other citizens

climate usual weather of a certain place

constitution plan for government

Continental Congress group of American colonists that met to win fair treatment from the British. On July 4, 1776, the Continental Congress signed the Declaration of Independence.

debt money owed to one person or group by another

diversity variety. A community with diversity has people of many different backgrounds, nationalities, interests, ages, and other characteristics.

Dutch East India Company powerful trading company that operated from about 1600 to about 1800

economy a country's use and production of money, goods, and services. The word *economic* describes anything having to do with the economy.

estuary place where a river flows into an ocean or sea

foundry place where metal is melted and molded into products

Hessian German soldier serving in the British army during the American Revolution

immigrant person who settles permanently in a foreign country

Industrial Revolution period when use of machines and the development of factories made it possible to produce more goods than ever before. The Industrial Revolution took place during the 1700s and 1800s.

industry group of businesses that offer a similar product or service

inlet small or narrow bay

internment camp place where Japanese Americans were imprisoned during World War II. The U.S. government believed they might be loyal to Japan rather than to the United States during the war.

iron ore rock and mineral material that contains iron

mammoth ancient long-haired elephant-like animal

melting pot term used for a country or other place where people of many nationalities or backgrounds live together

militia group of citizens organized for military service

mill building or group of buildings where a certain type of product is made

minutemen volunteer soldiers who fought in the American Revolution

monopoly control of a certain type of service or product in an area. When one company has a monopoly, no other companies can compete with it.

Paleo-Indians name given to the first people to live in North and South America

pelt furry skin of an animal that has been removed to make clothing or other articles

profit money made from business activities

proprietor person who owns something

prosperous making a lot of money

Puritan member of a religious group that split off from the Church of England in the 1500s. They created settlements in what is now Virginia and New England in the 1600s.

Quakers religious group that started in England in the 1600s. Quakers are known for their efforts to help all people by working for peace, education, and racial equality.

raw material product such as wood, minerals, cotton, animal hides, coal, and wool that are made into useful products in factories and mills

reservation land set aside by the government as a home for a group of people

shrewd clever

strike refuse to work in order to force an employer to offer higher wages or better working conditions

suburb city or town just outside a larger city. *Suburban* means having to do with a suburb

thrive to live well and grow quickly

treaty agreement between two governments or groups

Underground Railroad secret network that helped African American slaves escape to freedom in the North or in Canada

urban relating to the city

More Books to Read

Fredeen, Charles. *New Jersey.* Minneapolis, Minn.: Lerner Publishing Group, 2001.

Heinrichs, Ann. *New Jersey.* Minneapolis, Minn.: Compass Point Books, 2003.

Moragne, Wendy. *New Jersey.* Tarrytown, N.Y.: Marshall Cavendish Corporation, 2000.

Weatherly, Myra. *The New Jersey Colony.* Eden Prairie, Minn.: The Child's World, Inc., 2003.

Index

About the Author

Mark Stewart makes his home in New Jersey. A graduate of Duke University with a degree in history, Stewart has authored more than 100 nonfiction titles for the school and library market. He and his wife Sarah have two daughters, Mariah and Rachel.